45 Fruit Recipes for Home

By: Kelly Johnson

Table of Contents

- Classic Fruit Salad
- Mango Salsa
- Strawberry Spinach Salad
- Peach Caprese Salad
- Blueberry Lemon Pancakes
- Grilled Pineapple Chicken Skewers
- Raspberry Almond Tart
- Watermelon Feta Salad
- Homemade Apple Pie
- Kiwi Sorbet
- Orange Glazed Salmon
- Banana Bread
- Pineapple Fried Rice
- Grape and Goat Cheese Crostini
- Caramelized Fig and Prosciutto Pizza
- Mixed Berry Smoothie Bowl
- Lemon Blueberry Muffins
- Cherry Tomato Basil Bruschetta
- Passion Fruit Cheesecake
- Cranberry Orange Scones
- Mango Avocado Salsa
- Pear and Gorgonzola Salad
- Raspberry Chocolate Chip Cookies
- Peach BBQ Chicken Wings
- Lime Coconut Energy Bites
- Apple Cinnamon Overnight Oats
- Pomegranate Glazed Salmon
- Blackberry Mint Lemonade
- Caramel Apple Crisp
- Mango Chili Lime Chicken Tacos
- Pear Gingerbread Loaf
- Citrus Shrimp Skewers
- Blueberry Balsamic Glazed Chicken

- Apricot Glazed Pork Chops
- Mixed Fruit Galette
- Honeydew Basil Granita
- Pear and Walnut Salad
- Coconut Pineapple Popsicles
- Citrus Avocado Quinoa Salad
- Cherry Almond Clafoutis
- Lemon Raspberry Thumbprint Cookies
- Plum Ginger Chutney
- Blood Orange Sorbet
- Papaya Coconut Smoothie
- Cinnamon Sugar Baked Apples

Classic Fruit Salad

Ingredients:

- 2 cups fresh strawberries, hulled and halved
- 1 cup fresh blueberries
- 1 cup fresh grapes, halved
- 1 cup pineapple chunks
- 1 cup melon balls (cantaloupe and/or honeydew)
- 1 cup kiwi slices
- 1 banana, sliced
- 1 tablespoon honey (optional, for drizzling)
- Fresh mint leaves for garnish (optional)

Instructions:

Prepare the Fruits:
- Wash and prepare all the fruits as needed. Hull and halve the strawberries, halve the grapes, cut pineapple into chunks, create melon balls, slice kiwi, and cut the banana.

Combine Fruits:
- In a large mixing bowl, gently combine all the prepared fruits.

Drizzle with Honey (Optional):
- If you desire a touch of sweetness, drizzle honey over the fruit salad and gently toss to coat.

Chill:
- Cover the bowl with plastic wrap and refrigerate the fruit salad for at least 30 minutes to allow the flavors to meld and the salad to chill.

Serve:
- Before serving, give the fruit salad a gentle stir. Transfer to a serving bowl or individual dishes.

Garnish (Optional):
- Garnish with fresh mint leaves for a burst of freshness.

Enjoy:
- Serve this classic fruit salad as a refreshing side dish, snack, or dessert.

Note:

- Feel free to customize the fruit selection based on seasonal availability and personal preferences.
- Add a squeeze of fresh lime or lemon juice for a citrusy kick.
- This fruit salad is versatile and pairs well with yogurt or a dollop of whipped cream for a more indulgent treat.

Mango Salsa

Ingredients:

- 2 ripe mangoes, peeled, pitted, and diced
- 1 red bell pepper, finely chopped
- 1/2 red onion, finely chopped
- 1 jalapeño pepper, seeded and finely chopped
- 1/4 cup fresh cilantro, chopped
- 1 lime, juiced
- Salt and pepper to taste

Instructions:

Prepare Ingredients:
- Peel, pit, and dice the ripe mangoes. Finely chop the red bell pepper, red onion, jalapeño pepper, and fresh cilantro.

Combine Ingredients:
- In a mixing bowl, combine the diced mangoes, chopped red bell pepper, red onion, jalapeño pepper, and cilantro.

Add Lime Juice:
- Squeeze the juice of one lime over the mixture. Adjust the amount of lime juice to taste.

Season with Salt and Pepper:
- Season the mango salsa with salt and pepper, adjusting to your preference. Mix well to combine all the flavors.

Chill (Optional):
- For enhanced flavors, cover the bowl with plastic wrap and let the mango salsa chill in the refrigerator for at least 30 minutes before serving.

Serve:
- Serve the mango salsa as a topping for grilled chicken, fish, tacos, or as a refreshing dip with tortilla chips.

Enjoy:
- Enjoy the vibrant and flavorful mango salsa as a delicious and versatile addition to your meals.

Note:

- Experiment with additional ingredients like diced avocado, black beans, or corn for added texture and flavor.
- Adjust the spiciness by adding more or less jalapeño, or leave the seeds in for extra heat.
- This mango salsa is perfect for summer gatherings, barbecues, or as a simple snack.

Strawberry Spinach Salad

Ingredients:

For the Salad:

- 6 cups fresh baby spinach, washed and dried
- 2 cups fresh strawberries, hulled and sliced
- 1/2 cup red onion, thinly sliced
- 1/2 cup feta cheese, crumbled
- 1/2 cup candied pecans or walnuts, chopped

For the Dressing:

- 1/4 cup balsamic vinegar
- 1/4 cup extra-virgin olive oil
- 1 tablespoon Dijon mustard
- 1 tablespoon honey
- Salt and pepper to taste

Instructions:

Prepare the Salad:
- In a large salad bowl, combine the baby spinach, sliced strawberries, thinly sliced red onion, crumbled feta cheese, and chopped candied pecans or walnuts.

Make the Dressing:
- In a small bowl, whisk together the balsamic vinegar, olive oil, Dijon mustard, honey, salt, and pepper. Adjust the seasonings to your taste.

Dress the Salad:
- Drizzle the dressing over the salad, starting with a small amount. Toss the salad gently to coat the ingredients evenly.

Taste and Adjust:
- Taste the salad and adjust the dressing or seasoning as needed. Add more dressing if desired.

Serve:

- Transfer the Strawberry Spinach Salad to individual plates or a serving platter.

Optional Garnish:
- If desired, garnish the salad with additional crumbled feta or whole strawberries.

Enjoy:
- Serve immediately and enjoy the freshness and delightful combination of flavors in this Strawberry Spinach Salad.

Note:

- You can add grilled chicken or shrimp to make it a complete and satisfying main dish salad.
- Feel free to experiment with other nuts such as sliced almonds or sunflower seeds.
- This salad is perfect for spring and summer gatherings, bringing a burst of color and sweetness to the table.

Peach Caprese Salad

Ingredients:

- 3 ripe peaches, thinly sliced
- 1 pound fresh mozzarella, sliced
- Fresh basil leaves
- Balsamic glaze (store-bought or homemade)
- Extra-virgin olive oil
- Salt and pepper to taste

Instructions:

Slice Peaches and Mozzarella:
- Wash and thinly slice the ripe peaches. Similarly, slice the fresh mozzarella into rounds.

Assemble Salad:
- Arrange the peach slices and mozzarella slices alternately on a serving platter or individual plates.

Add Basil Leaves:
- Tuck fresh basil leaves between the peach and mozzarella slices. You can use whole leaves or chiffonade the basil for a finer texture.

Drizzle with Olive Oil:
- Drizzle extra-virgin olive oil over the peach and mozzarella slices. Use a good-quality olive oil for the best flavor.

Season with Salt and Pepper:
- Season the salad with salt and pepper to taste. Remember that the mozzarella will add some saltiness, so adjust accordingly.

Balsamic Glaze:
- Drizzle balsamic glaze over the Peach Caprese Salad. You can make a homemade balsamic reduction or use a store-bought balsamic glaze for convenience.

Serve:
- Serve the Peach Caprese Salad immediately, allowing the flavors to meld.

Enjoy:
- Enjoy this refreshing and elegant salad that combines the sweetness of peaches with the creamy texture of mozzarella and the aromatic freshness of basil.

Note:

- You can customize this salad by adding prosciutto slices for a savory twist or arugula for a peppery bite.
- Adjust the sweetness of the salad by choosing peaches that are perfectly ripe and juicy.
- This Peach Caprese Salad is a beautiful appetizer or side dish, ideal for summer gatherings or as a light lunch.

Blueberry Lemon Pancakes

Ingredients:

- 1 cup all-purpose flour
- 2 tablespoons granulated sugar
- 1 teaspoon baking powder
- 1/2 teaspoon baking soda
- 1/4 teaspoon salt
- 1 cup buttermilk
- 1 large egg
- 2 tablespoons unsalted butter, melted
- Zest of 1 lemon
- 1 cup fresh blueberries
- Butter or cooking spray for greasing the griddle

Instructions:

Preheat Griddle or Pan:
- Preheat a griddle or non-stick pan over medium heat.

Prepare Dry Ingredients:
- In a large mixing bowl, whisk together the flour, sugar, baking powder, baking soda, and salt.

Combine Wet Ingredients:
- In a separate bowl, whisk together the buttermilk, egg, melted butter, and lemon zest.

Mix Batter:
- Pour the wet ingredients into the dry ingredients and stir until just combined. Be careful not to overmix; it's okay if there are a few lumps.

Fold in Blueberries:
- Gently fold in the fresh blueberries into the pancake batter.

Grease Griddle:
- Grease the griddle or pan with butter or cooking spray.

Spoon Batter onto Griddle:
- Using a 1/4 cup measuring cup, spoon the batter onto the preheated griddle to form pancakes.

Cook until Bubbles Form:

- Cook the pancakes until bubbles form on the surface and the edges start to look set.

Flip and Cook Other Side:
- Carefully flip the pancakes with a spatula and cook the other side until golden brown.

Repeat:
- Repeat the process with the remaining batter.

Serve:
- Serve the Blueberry Lemon Pancakes warm with your favorite syrup, additional blueberries, and a dusting of powdered sugar if desired.

Enjoy:
- Enjoy these light and fluffy pancakes bursting with the sweetness of blueberries and the citrusy zing of lemon!

Note:

- For extra lemon flavor, you can add a teaspoon of lemon juice to the wet ingredients.
- If fresh blueberries are not available, you can use frozen blueberries. Just be sure not to thaw them before folding into the batter.
- Adjust the sweetness by adding more or less sugar to the batter based on your preference.

Grilled Pineapple Chicken Skewers

Ingredients:

For the Marinade:

- 1/4 cup soy sauce
- 2 tablespoons honey
- 2 tablespoons olive oil
- 2 cloves garlic, minced
- 1 teaspoon ginger, grated
- 1 teaspoon smoked paprika
- Salt and pepper to taste

For the Skewers:

- 1.5 pounds boneless, skinless chicken breasts, cut into cubes
- 1 pineapple, peeled, cored, and cut into chunks
- Bell peppers, cherry tomatoes, or red onion (optional, for additional skewer ingredients)

Instructions:

Prepare Marinade:
- In a bowl, whisk together soy sauce, honey, olive oil, minced garlic, grated ginger, smoked paprika, salt, and pepper.

Marinate Chicken:
- Place the chicken cubes in a zip-top bag or shallow dish. Pour half of the marinade over the chicken, ensuring it is well-coated. Reserve the remaining marinade for basting.

Marinate Pineapple:
- In a separate bowl, toss the pineapple chunks in a portion of the marinade to coat evenly.

Marinate for at Least 30 Minutes:
- Seal the bags or cover the dishes and marinate in the refrigerator for at least 30 minutes, or preferably 2-4 hours for more flavor.

Preheat Grill:
- Preheat the grill to medium-high heat.

Assemble Skewers:

- Thread the marinated chicken and pineapple chunks onto skewers, alternating between them. If desired, add bell peppers, cherry tomatoes, or red onion between the chicken and pineapple.

Grill Skewers:
- Place the skewers on the preheated grill. Cook for about 12-15 minutes, turning occasionally, until the chicken is fully cooked and has a nice char.

Baste with Reserved Marinade:
- During the last few minutes of grilling, baste the skewers with the reserved marinade for extra flavor.

Serve:
- Once the chicken is cooked through and has a nice grill mark, remove the skewers from the grill.

Garnish (Optional):
- Garnish with chopped cilantro or parsley if desired.

Enjoy:
- Serve the Grilled Pineapple Chicken Skewers hot, and enjoy the delicious combination of savory, sweet, and smoky flavors!

Note:

- Soak wooden skewers in water for 30 minutes before threading to prevent them from burning on the grill.
- Feel free to customize the skewers with your favorite vegetables or additional fruits for added variety.
- Serve these skewers over rice, quinoa, or a bed of greens for a complete meal.

Raspberry Almond Tart

Ingredients:

For the Almond Crust:

- 1 cup all-purpose flour
- 1/2 cup almond flour
- 1/4 cup granulated sugar
- 1/2 cup unsalted butter, cold and cut into small cubes
- 1 large egg yolk
- 1-2 tablespoons ice water (if needed)

For the Almond Filling:

- 1 cup almond flour
- 1/2 cup granulated sugar
- 1/3 cup unsalted butter, softened
- 1 large egg
- 1 teaspoon almond extract

For the Topping:

- 2 cups fresh raspberries
- 2 tablespoons apricot preserves (for glaze)
- Sliced almonds for garnish (optional)

Instructions:

Preheat Oven:
- Preheat the oven to 375°F (190°C).

Prepare Almond Crust:
- In a food processor, combine the all-purpose flour, almond flour, sugar, and cold butter. Pulse until the mixture resembles coarse crumbs.

Add Egg Yolk:
- Add the egg yolk and pulse again until the dough starts to come together. If needed, add 1-2 tablespoons of ice water to help bind the dough.

Form Dough:

- Turn the dough out onto a floured surface and gently knead it into a ball. Flatten into a disk, wrap in plastic wrap, and refrigerate for at least 30 minutes.

Roll Out Crust:
- On a floured surface, roll out the chilled dough to fit a tart pan. Press the dough into the bottom and up the sides of the tart pan. Trim any excess.

Prepare Almond Filling:
- In a bowl, mix together almond flour, sugar, softened butter, egg, and almond extract until well combined.

Spread Almond Filling:
- Spread the almond filling evenly over the prepared crust.

Bake:
- Bake the tart crust with almond filling in the preheated oven for about 20-25 minutes or until the edges are golden brown.

Cool:
- Allow the crust and filling to cool completely before proceeding.

Arrange Raspberries:
- Arrange fresh raspberries on top of the almond filling in a decorative pattern.

Make Apricot Glaze:
- In a small saucepan, heat apricot preserves over low heat until melted. Strain to remove any solids.

Brush with Glaze:
- Brush the raspberry topping with the apricot glaze for a shiny finish.

Optional Garnish:
- Sprinkle sliced almonds over the top for an optional garnish.

Chill (Optional):
- For a firmer tart, chill in the refrigerator for an hour before serving.

Slice and Serve:
- Slice and serve this delightful Raspberry Almond Tart. Enjoy!

Note:

- You can use a 9-inch tart pan with a removable bottom for easy serving.
- Experiment with other fresh berries or fruits for a variation in flavors and colors.
- Dust the tart with powdered sugar before serving for an extra touch.

Watermelon Feta Salad

Ingredients:

- 4 cups seedless watermelon, diced into bite-sized cubes
- 1 cup feta cheese, crumbled
- 1 cup cucumber, diced
- 1/4 cup red onion, thinly sliced
- 1/4 cup fresh mint leaves, chopped
- 1/4 cup extra-virgin olive oil
- 2 tablespoons balsamic glaze
- Salt and black pepper to taste

Instructions:

Prepare Watermelon:
- Remove the rind and seeds from the watermelon, and dice it into bite-sized cubes.

Combine Ingredients:
- In a large mixing bowl, combine the diced watermelon, crumbled feta cheese, diced cucumber, thinly sliced red onion, and chopped fresh mint.

Make Dressing:
- In a small bowl, whisk together the extra-virgin olive oil and balsamic glaze to create a simple dressing.

Drizzle Dressing:
- Drizzle the dressing over the watermelon mixture. Gently toss the salad until all ingredients are coated.

Season with Salt and Pepper:
- Season the salad with salt and black pepper to taste. Remember that feta cheese can add a salty flavor, so adjust accordingly.

Chill (Optional):
- If time allows, refrigerate the Watermelon Feta Salad for about 15-30 minutes to enhance the flavors and chill the ingredients.

Serve:
- Transfer the salad to a serving platter or individual dishes.

Garnish (Optional):
- Garnish with additional fresh mint leaves for a pop of color.

Enjoy:

- Serve immediately and enjoy the refreshing combination of sweet watermelon, salty feta, and crisp vegetables.

Note:

- Customize the salad by adding Kalamata olives, cherry tomatoes, or arugula for additional flavors and textures.
- Drizzle a little extra balsamic glaze over the top just before serving for a finishing touch.
- This Watermelon Feta Salad is perfect for summer picnics, barbecues, or as a light and hydrating side dish.

Homemade Apple Pie

Ingredients:

For the Pie Crust:

- 2 1/2 cups all-purpose flour
- 1 cup unsalted butter, cold and cut into small cubes
- 1 teaspoon salt
- 1 tablespoon granulated sugar
- 1/2 cup ice water

For the Apple Filling:

- 6-7 medium-sized apples (a mix of sweet and tart varieties like Granny Smith and Honeycrisp), peeled, cored, and thinly sliced
- 1/2 cup granulated sugar
- 1/2 cup light brown sugar, packed
- 1 teaspoon ground cinnamon
- 1/4 teaspoon ground nutmeg
- 1/4 teaspoon salt
- 2 tablespoons all-purpose flour
- 1 tablespoon lemon juice

For Assembly and Topping:

- 1 tablespoon unsalted butter, cut into small pieces (for dotting the filling)
- 1 egg, beaten (for egg wash)
- 1 tablespoon granulated sugar (for sprinkling over the crust)

Instructions:

Prepare Pie Crust:
- In a food processor, pulse the flour, salt, and sugar until combined. Add the cold, cubed butter and pulse until the mixture resembles coarse crumbs. Gradually add the ice water, one tablespoon at a time, and pulse until the dough comes together.

Form Dough:
- Divide the dough in half, form each half into a disk, wrap in plastic wrap, and refrigerate for at least 1 hour.

Preheat Oven:
- Preheat the oven to 375°F (190°C).

Roll Out Dough:
- On a floured surface, roll out one disk of the chilled pie crust to fit a 9-inch pie dish. Place it into the pie dish and trim any excess hanging over the edges.

Prepare Apple Filling:
- In a large bowl, toss the sliced apples with granulated sugar, brown sugar, cinnamon, nutmeg, salt, flour, and lemon juice until well coated.

Fill Pie Crust:
- Pour the apple filling into the prepared pie crust, dot the top with small pieces of butter.

Roll Out Second Dough:
- Roll out the second disk of pie crust and place it over the apple filling. Trim any excess and crimp the edges to seal the pie.

Cut Slits:
- Cut a few slits in the top crust to allow steam to escape during baking.

Brush with Egg Wash:
- Brush the top crust with the beaten egg and sprinkle with granulated sugar for a golden finish.

Bake:
- Place the pie on a baking sheet and bake in the preheated oven for 45-55 minutes or until the crust is golden brown and the filling is bubbly.

Cool:
- Allow the pie to cool completely on a wire rack before slicing.

Serve:
- Serve your Homemade Apple Pie with a scoop of vanilla ice cream or a dollop of whipped cream.

Enjoy:
- Enjoy this classic and comforting dessert!

Note:

- Make sure to use cold ingredients for the pie crust to achieve a flaky texture.
- Adjust the sugar in the filling based on your preference and the sweetness of the apples.
- Feel free to add a pinch of cloves or ginger to the filling for extra warmth and flavor.

Kiwi Sorbet

Ingredients:

- 5-6 ripe kiwi fruit, peeled and sliced
- 1/2 cup granulated sugar (adjust according to taste)
- 1/4 cup water
- 1-2 tablespoons fresh lime or lemon juice

Instructions:

Prepare Kiwi:
- Peel the kiwi fruit and slice them into small pieces.

Make Simple Syrup:
- In a small saucepan, combine the granulated sugar and water. Heat over medium heat, stirring until the sugar dissolves. Bring it to a simmer and then remove it from heat. Allow the simple syrup to cool.

Blend Kiwi:
- In a blender or food processor, blend the sliced kiwi until smooth.

Strain (Optional):
- If you prefer a smoother sorbet, you can strain the kiwi puree using a fine-mesh sieve to remove the seeds.

Combine with Simple Syrup:
- In a bowl, combine the kiwi puree with the cooled simple syrup. Mix well.

Add Lime or Lemon Juice:
- Stir in fresh lime or lemon juice to enhance the flavor. Adjust the amount according to your taste preference.

Chill Mixture:
- Place the mixture in the refrigerator for at least 2-3 hours, allowing it to chill thoroughly.

Freeze:
- Transfer the chilled kiwi mixture into an ice cream maker and churn according to the manufacturer's instructions until it reaches a sorbet-like consistency.

Serve or Freeze:
- You can serve the kiwi sorbet immediately for a soft-serve texture, or transfer it to a lidded container and freeze for a firmer texture.

Enjoy:

- Scoop the Kiwi Sorbet into bowls or cones, and enjoy this refreshing and tangy frozen treat!

Note:

- Adjust the sugar and lime/lemon juice according to the sweetness and tartness of the kiwi fruit.
- If you don't have an ice cream maker, you can pour the mixture into a lidded container and freeze, stirring every 30 minutes until it reaches the desired consistency.
- Garnish with kiwi slices or mint leaves for an extra touch when serving.

Orange Glazed Salmon

Ingredients:

- 4 salmon fillets
- Salt and black pepper to taste
- 2 tablespoons olive oil

For the Orange Glaze:

- 1/2 cup fresh orange juice
- Zest of 1 orange
- 2 tablespoons soy sauce
- 2 tablespoons honey
- 1 tablespoon Dijon mustard
- 1 teaspoon minced garlic
- 1 teaspoon grated ginger
- 1 tablespoon cornstarch (optional, for thickening)

Instructions:

Preheat Oven:
- Preheat your oven to 400°F (200°C).

Season Salmon:
- Season the salmon fillets with salt and black pepper.

Sear Salmon:
- In an oven-safe skillet, heat olive oil over medium-high heat. Sear the salmon fillets, skin side down, for 2-3 minutes until golden brown.

Make Orange Glaze:
- In a bowl, whisk together fresh orange juice, orange zest, soy sauce, honey, Dijon mustard, minced garlic, and grated ginger to create the orange glaze.

Coat Salmon:
- Pour half of the orange glaze over the seared salmon fillets, coating them evenly.

Bake:
- Transfer the skillet to the preheated oven and bake for 10-12 minutes or until the salmon is cooked through and flakes easily with a fork.

Thicken Glaze (Optional):

- If you prefer a thicker glaze, mix cornstarch with a little water to create a slurry. Add it to the remaining half of the orange glaze and cook on the stovetop until it thickens.

Finish with Glaze:
- Once the salmon is cooked, brush the remaining thickened glaze over the fillets.

Serve:
- Serve the Orange Glazed Salmon over rice, quinoa, or your preferred side dish. Drizzle any remaining glaze over the top.

Garnish (Optional):
- Garnish with chopped green onions or fresh parsley for a burst of color and flavor.

Enjoy:
- Enjoy this delicious and flavorful Orange Glazed Salmon with the perfect balance of citrusy sweetness and savory notes!

Note:

- Adjust the sweetness and saltiness of the glaze according to your taste preferences.
- You can also grill the salmon instead of baking it for a different cooking method.
- Serve with steamed vegetables or a side salad for a complete meal.

Banana Bread

Ingredients:

- 3 ripe bananas, mashed
- 1/2 cup unsalted butter, melted
- 1 teaspoon vanilla extract
- 1/2 cup granulated sugar
- 1/2 cup brown sugar, packed
- 2 large eggs
- 1 3/4 cups all-purpose flour
- 1 teaspoon baking soda
- 1/2 teaspoon salt
- 1/2 teaspoon ground cinnamon (optional)
- 1/2 cup chopped nuts or chocolate chips (optional)

Instructions:

Preheat Oven:
- Preheat your oven to 350°F (175°C). Grease and flour a 9x5-inch loaf pan.

Mash Bananas:
- In a mixing bowl, mash the ripe bananas with a fork or potato masher until smooth.

Combine Wet Ingredients:
- Add melted butter, vanilla extract, granulated sugar, brown sugar, and eggs to the mashed bananas. Mix until well combined.

Sift Dry Ingredients:
- In a separate bowl, sift together the flour, baking soda, salt, and ground cinnamon (if using).

Combine Wet and Dry Ingredients:
- Gradually add the dry ingredients to the wet ingredients, stirring until just combined. Do not overmix.

Add Nuts or Chocolate (Optional):
- If desired, fold in chopped nuts or chocolate chips into the batter.

Pour into Pan:
- Pour the batter into the prepared loaf pan, spreading it evenly.

Bake:
- Bake in the preheated oven for 60-70 minutes or until a toothpick inserted into the center comes out clean or with a few moist crumbs.

Cool:
- Allow the banana bread to cool in the pan for about 10 minutes before transferring it to a wire rack to cool completely.

Slice and Serve:
- Once cooled, slice the banana bread and serve. It's delicious on its own or with a spread of butter.

Store:
- Store any leftover banana bread in an airtight container at room temperature for up to 3 days, or refrigerate for longer freshness.

Enjoy:
- Enjoy this classic and moist banana bread with your favorite cup of coffee or tea!

Note:

- Feel free to customize the banana bread by adding extras like nuts, chocolate chips, or dried fruits.
- If your bananas aren't ripe enough, you can place them in the oven at 300°F (150°C) for 15-20 minutes until the peels turn black.
- Adjust the sweetness by using more or less sugar, depending on your preference.

Pineapple Fried Rice

Ingredients:

- 3 cups cooked jasmine rice (preferably cooled or day-old)
- 1 cup pineapple chunks, fresh or canned
- 1 cup diced cooked chicken, shrimp, or tofu (optional)
- 1/2 cup peas, fresh or frozen
- 1/2 cup diced carrots
- 1/2 cup chopped bell peppers (any color)
- 3 green onions, sliced
- 3 tablespoons soy sauce
- 1 tablespoon fish sauce (optional for umami flavor)
- 1 tablespoon oyster sauce
- 2 tablespoons vegetable oil
- 2 cloves garlic, minced
- 2 eggs, lightly beaten
- 1/4 cup chopped cilantro (optional for garnish)
- Lime wedges for serving

Instructions:

Prep Ingredients:
- Ensure that all ingredients are chopped and ready before you start cooking.

Heat Oil:
- In a large wok or skillet, heat the vegetable oil over medium-high heat.

Cook Garlic and Eggs:
- Add minced garlic to the hot oil and sauté for about 30 seconds until fragrant. Push the garlic to the side and pour the beaten eggs into the pan. Scramble the eggs until just cooked.

Add Protein (Optional):
- If using chicken, shrimp, or tofu, add it to the pan and cook until the protein is fully cooked.

Add Vegetables:
- Add diced carrots, bell peppers, and peas to the pan. Stir-fry for 2-3 minutes until the vegetables are slightly tender.

Add Rice:

- Add the cooked jasmine rice to the pan, breaking up any clumps. Stir well to combine with the vegetables and protein.

Add Pineapple:
- Add pineapple chunks to the rice mixture. Stir to distribute evenly.

Combine Sauces:
- In a small bowl, mix soy sauce, fish sauce (if using), and oyster sauce. Pour the sauce over the rice mixture and stir to coat everything evenly.

Add Green Onions:
- Add sliced green onions to the pan and toss until well combined.

Adjust Seasoning:
- Taste the fried rice and adjust the seasoning if needed. You can add more soy sauce or a dash of salt if desired.

Garnish (Optional):
- If desired, garnish the pineapple fried rice with chopped cilantro for freshness.

Serve:
- Serve the pineapple fried rice hot, with lime wedges on the side for squeezing over the rice.

Enjoy:
- Enjoy this delicious and colorful Pineapple Fried Rice as a main dish or as a flavorful side!

Note:

- Feel free to customize the ingredients by adding cashews, raisins, or other vegetables of your choice.
- Use day-old rice or rice that has been chilled for better texture and to prevent it from becoming mushy during cooking.

Grape and Goat Cheese Crostini

Ingredients:

- Baguette, sliced into 1/2-inch thick rounds
- 1 tablespoon olive oil
- 1 cup red or black grapes, halved
- 4 ounces goat cheese, softened
- 2 tablespoons honey
- Fresh thyme leaves for garnish
- Balsamic glaze (optional)

Instructions:

Preheat Oven:
- Preheat the oven to 375°F (190°C).

Brush Baguette Slices:
- Place the baguette slices on a baking sheet. Brush each slice with olive oil.

Bake Baguette:
- Bake the baguette slices in the preheated oven for 8-10 minutes or until they are golden and crispy.

Prepare Grapes:
- While the baguette slices are baking, halve the grapes.

Spread Goat Cheese:
- Once the baguette slices are out of the oven, spread a generous layer of softened goat cheese on each slice.

Add Grapes:
- Top each crostini with halved grapes, pressing them slightly into the goat cheese.

Drizzle with Honey:
- Drizzle honey over the grape and goat cheese-topped crostinis.

Garnish:
- Garnish the crostinis with fresh thyme leaves for added flavor and a pop of color.

Optional Balsamic Glaze:
- If desired, drizzle a small amount of balsamic glaze over the crostinis for a tangy and sweet touch.

Serve:

- Arrange the Grape and Goat Cheese Crostini on a serving platter.

Enjoy:
- Serve immediately and enjoy this delightful combination of sweet grapes, creamy goat cheese, and honey on crispy crostini.

Note:

- You can customize this recipe by using different types of grapes or adding a sprinkle of chopped nuts like walnuts or pistachios for added crunch.
- The balsamic glaze is optional but adds a nice depth of flavor. Adjust the amount to your taste preference.
- Fresh rosemary or mint leaves can be used instead of thyme for a different herbal flavor.

Caramelized Fig and Prosciutto Pizza

Ingredients:

- Pizza dough (store-bought or homemade)
- 1/2 cup fig jam or preserves
- 1 cup fresh figs, sliced
- 6 slices prosciutto
- 1 cup mozzarella cheese, shredded
- 1/4 cup goat cheese, crumbled
- 1 tablespoon balsamic glaze
- Arugula for garnish
- Olive oil for drizzling

Instructions:

Preheat Oven:
- Preheat your oven to the temperature recommended for your pizza dough.

Roll Out Pizza Dough:
- Roll out the pizza dough on a floured surface to your desired thickness.

Prepare Pizza Stone or Pan:
- If using a pizza stone, place it in the oven to heat. If using a baking sheet, lightly grease it.

Transfer Dough:
- Transfer the rolled-out pizza dough onto a pizza peel or another inverted baking sheet if using a stone. If using a baking sheet, place the rolled-out dough directly onto it.

Spread Fig Jam:
- Spread a layer of fig jam or preserves evenly over the pizza dough, leaving a small border around the edges.

Add Mozzarella and Goat Cheese:
- Sprinkle shredded mozzarella over the fig jam. Dot the pizza with crumbled goat cheese.

Arrange Figs and Prosciutto:
- Arrange the sliced fresh figs and prosciutto evenly over the cheese.

Bake:
- Transfer the pizza to the preheated oven (or onto the hot pizza stone) and bake according to the pizza dough instructions or until the crust is golden and the cheese is melted and bubbly.

Drizzle with Balsamic Glaze:
- Once out of the oven, drizzle the pizza with balsamic glaze for a sweet and tangy finish.

Garnish with Arugula:
- Scatter fresh arugula over the hot pizza. The heat will wilt the arugula slightly.

Drizzle with Olive Oil:
- Finish the pizza with a drizzle of olive oil for added richness and flavor.

Slice and Serve:
- Slice the Caramelized Fig and Prosciutto Pizza into wedges and serve immediately.

Enjoy:
- Enjoy this gourmet pizza with the perfect balance of sweet and savory flavors!

Note:

- You can add a handful of shaved Parmesan or Pecorino cheese on top before serving for an extra layer of richness.
- Experiment with different types of figs or use dried figs if fresh ones are not available.
- The arugula can be tossed in a light vinaigrette before adding it to the pizza for extra flavor.

Mixed Berry Smoothie Bowl

Ingredients:

For the Smoothie:

- 1 cup frozen mixed berries (strawberries, blueberries, raspberries, blackberries)
- 1 ripe banana, frozen
- 1/2 cup plain Greek yogurt
- 1/2 cup almond milk (or any milk of your choice)
- 1 tablespoon honey or maple syrup (optional for sweetness)

For Toppings:

- Fresh berries (strawberries, blueberries, raspberries, blackberries)
- Granola
- Chia seeds
- Sliced banana
- Shredded coconut
- Nut butter (almond butter, peanut butter)
- Edible flowers (optional, for decoration)

Instructions:

Prepare Smoothie Base:
- In a blender, combine frozen mixed berries, frozen banana, Greek yogurt, almond milk, and honey or maple syrup if using. Blend until smooth and creamy.

Adjust Consistency:
- If the smoothie is too thick, add a bit more almond milk. If it's too thin, add more frozen berries or banana to thicken.

Pour into Bowl:
- Pour the mixed berry smoothie into a bowl.

Arrange Toppings:
- Arrange fresh berries, granola, chia seeds, sliced banana, shredded coconut, and a drizzle of nut butter on top of the smoothie.

Decorate (Optional):
- If desired, add edible flowers for a decorative touch.

Serve Immediately:

- Serve the Mixed Berry Smoothie Bowl immediately and enjoy with a spoon!

Note:

- Feel free to customize the toppings based on your preferences. Other options include sliced almonds, hemp seeds, or a sprinkle of cinnamon.
- For an extra nutritional boost, add a handful of spinach or kale to the smoothie base (this may affect the color but not the taste).
- Experiment with different milk alternatives such as coconut milk, soy milk, or oat milk.
- Adjust the sweetness of the smoothie by varying the amount of honey or maple syrup according to your taste.

Lemon Blueberry Muffins

Ingredients:

- 2 cups all-purpose flour
- 1 cup granulated sugar
- 1 tablespoon baking powder
- 1/2 teaspoon baking soda
- 1/4 teaspoon salt
- 1 cup blueberries (fresh or frozen)
- Zest of 1 lemon
- 1/4 cup fresh lemon juice
- 1/2 cup unsalted butter, melted and cooled
- 2 large eggs
- 1 teaspoon vanilla extract
- 1 cup plain Greek yogurt

For the Lemon Glaze:

- 1 cup powdered sugar
- 2-3 tablespoons fresh lemon juice
- Zest of 1 lemon (optional, for extra flavor)

Instructions:

Preheat Oven:
- Preheat your oven to 375°F (190°C). Line a muffin tin with paper liners or grease the cups.

Combine Dry Ingredients:
- In a large mixing bowl, whisk together the flour, sugar, baking powder, baking soda, and salt.

Add Blueberries and Lemon Zest:
- Gently fold in the blueberries and lemon zest until the blueberries are coated with the flour mixture.

Prepare Wet Ingredients:
- In a separate bowl, whisk together the melted butter, lemon juice, eggs, vanilla extract, and Greek yogurt.

Combine Wet and Dry Ingredients:

- Pour the wet ingredients into the bowl with the dry ingredients. Stir until just combined. Do not overmix; it's okay if there are a few lumps.

Fill Muffin Cups:
- Spoon the batter into the prepared muffin cups, filling each about 2/3 full.

Bake:
- Bake in the preheated oven for 18-20 minutes or until a toothpick inserted into the center of a muffin comes out clean or with a few moist crumbs.

Cool:
- Allow the muffins to cool in the tin for 5 minutes before transferring them to a wire rack to cool completely.

Prepare Lemon Glaze:
- In a small bowl, whisk together the powdered sugar and lemon juice to create the glaze. Add more or less lemon juice to achieve your desired consistency.

Drizzle Glaze:
- Drizzle the lemon glaze over the cooled muffins.

Optional Lemon Zest Garnish:
- If desired, sprinkle additional lemon zest over the glaze for extra flavor and a decorative touch.

Serve and Enjoy:
- Serve the Lemon Blueberry Muffins and enjoy these delightful, citrus-infused treats!

Note:

- If using frozen blueberries, toss them in a bit of flour before adding them to the batter to help prevent them from sinking to the bottom.
- Adjust the amount of lemon juice in the glaze to suit your taste preference.
- These muffins are best enjoyed on the day they are baked, but you can store leftovers in an airtight container for a day or two.

Cherry Tomato Basil Bruschetta

Ingredients:

- 1 pint cherry tomatoes, halved
- 1/4 cup fresh basil, finely chopped
- 2 cloves garlic, minced
- 1 tablespoon balsamic vinegar
- 2 tablespoons extra-virgin olive oil
- Salt and black pepper to taste
- Baguette or Italian bread, sliced
- 1 garlic clove, peeled (for rubbing on bread)

Instructions:

Prepare Tomatoes and Basil:
- Wash and halve the cherry tomatoes. Finely chop the fresh basil.

Make Bruschetta Mixture:
- In a bowl, combine the cherry tomatoes, chopped basil, minced garlic, balsamic vinegar, and extra-virgin olive oil. Mix well to coat the tomatoes and basil evenly. Season with salt and black pepper to taste.

Let It Marinate:
- Allow the bruschetta mixture to marinate for at least 15-20 minutes to let the flavors meld.

Toast Bread Slices:
- While the bruschetta is marinating, toast the slices of baguette or Italian bread. You can do this in a toaster, on a grill, or in the oven.

Rub Bread with Garlic:
- Once the bread slices are toasted, rub each slice with a peeled garlic clove. This adds a subtle garlic flavor to the bread.

Top with Bruschetta Mixture:
- Spoon the marinated cherry tomato and basil mixture generously over each garlic-rubbed bread slice.

Serve:
- Arrange the Cherry Tomato Basil Bruschetta on a serving platter and serve immediately.

Enjoy:
- Enjoy this fresh and flavorful appetizer as a light snack or as a prelude to an Italian-inspired meal!

Note:

- You can customize the bruschetta by adding a drizzle of balsamic glaze or a sprinkle of grated Parmesan cheese on top.
- If you prefer a more intense garlic flavor, you can mix minced garlic directly into the bruschetta mixture.
- Experiment with different types of bread, such as ciabatta or sourdough, for variety.

Passion Fruit Cheesecake

Ingredients:

For the Crust:

- 1 1/2 cups graham cracker crumbs
- 1/3 cup unsalted butter, melted
- 2 tablespoons granulated sugar

For the Cheesecake Filling:

- 4 packages (32 ounces) cream cheese, softened
- 1 1/4 cups granulated sugar
- 4 large eggs
- 1 cup sour cream
- 1/2 cup passion fruit puree (strained if seeds are present)
- 1 teaspoon vanilla extract
- Zest of 1 lemon

For the Passion Fruit Glaze:

- 1/2 cup passion fruit puree
- 1/4 cup granulated sugar
- 1 tablespoon cornstarch
- 1/4 cup water

Instructions:

Preheat Oven:
- Preheat your oven to 325°F (163°C). Grease the bottom and sides of a 9-inch springform pan.

Prepare Crust:
- In a bowl, combine graham cracker crumbs, melted butter, and sugar. Press the mixture into the bottom of the prepared springform pan to form the crust.

Bake Crust:
- Bake the crust in the preheated oven for 10 minutes. Remove and let it cool while preparing the filling.

Prepare Cheesecake Filling:

- In a large mixing bowl, beat the softened cream cheese and sugar until smooth and creamy. Add eggs one at a time, beating well after each addition.

Add Sour Cream and Flavorings:
- Mix in the sour cream, passion fruit puree, vanilla extract, and lemon zest until well combined.

Pour Filling Over Crust:
- Pour the cheesecake filling over the cooled crust in the springform pan.

Bake Cheesecake:
- Bake the cheesecake in the preheated oven for 60-70 minutes or until the center is set, and the top is lightly browned.

Cool and Refrigerate:
- Allow the cheesecake to cool in the pan on a wire rack. Once cooled, refrigerate for at least 4 hours or overnight to set.

Prepare Passion Fruit Glaze:
- In a small saucepan, combine passion fruit puree, sugar, cornstarch, and water. Cook over medium heat, stirring constantly until the mixture thickens.

Cool Glaze:
- Let the passion fruit glaze cool to room temperature.

Pour Glaze Over Cheesecake:
- Pour the cooled passion fruit glaze over the chilled cheesecake, spreading it evenly.

Chill Again:
- Return the cheesecake to the refrigerator and chill for an additional 2 hours to allow the glaze to set.

Serve:
- Carefully remove the sides of the springform pan. Slice and serve the delectable Passion Fruit Cheesecake.

Enjoy:
- Enjoy this tropical-inspired cheesecake with the unique and vibrant flavor of passion fruit!

Note:

- Ensure that all ingredients are at room temperature to achieve a smooth and creamy cheesecake texture.
- Straining the passion fruit puree can help remove seeds for a smoother consistency in both the filling and glaze.

- Adjust the sweetness of the glaze according to your preference by adding more or less sugar.

Cranberry Orange Scones

Ingredients:

For the Scones:

- 2 cups all-purpose flour
- 1/4 cup granulated sugar
- 1 tablespoon baking powder
- 1/2 teaspoon salt
- 1/2 cup unsalted butter, cold and cut into small pieces
- 1/2 cup dried cranberries
- Zest of 1 orange
- 2/3 cup whole milk or heavy cream
- 1 teaspoon vanilla extract

For the Orange Glaze:

- 1 cup powdered sugar
- 2 tablespoons fresh orange juice
- Zest of 1 orange

Instructions:

Preheat Oven:
- Preheat your oven to 400°F (200°C). Line a baking sheet with parchment paper.

Prepare Scone Dough:
- In a large mixing bowl, whisk together flour, sugar, baking powder, and salt. Add cold, cubed butter, and using a pastry cutter or your fingertips, cut the butter into the flour mixture until it resembles coarse crumbs.

Add Cranberries and Orange Zest:
- Stir in the dried cranberries and orange zest.

Combine Wet Ingredients:
- In a separate bowl, mix together milk or heavy cream and vanilla extract.

Form Dough:
- Make a well in the center of the dry ingredients, pour in the wet ingredients, and gently stir until just combined. Do not overmix.

Knead and Shape:

- Turn the dough out onto a lightly floured surface. Gently knead it a few times until it comes together. Pat the dough into a circle about 1 inch thick.

Cut into Wedges:
- Using a sharp knife, cut the dough into 8 equal wedges.

Arrange on Baking Sheet:
- Place the scones on the prepared baking sheet, leaving some space between each wedge.

Bake:
- Bake in the preheated oven for 15-18 minutes or until the scones are golden brown and cooked through.

Prepare Orange Glaze:
- While the scones are baking, prepare the orange glaze. In a bowl, whisk together powdered sugar, fresh orange juice, and orange zest until smooth.

Glaze Scones:
- Once the scones are out of the oven and slightly cooled, drizzle the orange glaze over the top of each scone.

Cool and Serve:
- Allow the glaze to set, and then transfer the scones to a wire rack to cool completely.

Enjoy:
- Enjoy these Cranberry Orange Scones with a cup of tea or coffee for a delightful treat!

Note:

- For an extra burst of citrus flavor, you can add a few drops of orange extract to the scone dough.
- If you prefer a different glaze consistency, adjust the amount of orange juice in the glaze accordingly.
- Store any leftover scones in an airtight container at room temperature for up to 2 days or in the refrigerator for longer freshness.

Mango Avocado Salsa

Ingredients:

- 1 ripe mango, diced
- 1 ripe avocado, diced
- 1/2 cup red onion, finely chopped
- 1/2 cup cherry tomatoes, halved
- 1/4 cup fresh cilantro, chopped
- 1 jalapeño, seeded and finely diced
- Juice of 1 lime
- Salt and pepper to taste

Instructions:

Prepare Ingredients:
- Dice the ripe mango and avocado. Finely chop the red onion and fresh cilantro. Halve the cherry tomatoes. Seed and finely dice the jalapeño.

Combine Ingredients:
- In a mixing bowl, combine the diced mango, diced avocado, chopped red onion, halved cherry tomatoes, chopped cilantro, and diced jalapeño.

Squeeze Lime Juice:
- Squeeze the juice of one lime over the ingredients. Adjust the amount of lime juice to your taste preference.

Season with Salt and Pepper:
- Season the salsa with salt and pepper to taste. Mix gently to combine all the ingredients.

Chill (Optional):
- If time allows, let the salsa chill in the refrigerator for about 15-30 minutes to allow the flavors to meld.

Serve:
- Serve the Mango Avocado Salsa as a refreshing and flavorful topping for grilled chicken, fish, tacos, or simply with tortilla chips.

Enjoy:
- Enjoy this vibrant and delicious salsa with the sweet and creamy combination of mango and avocado!

Note:

- Customize the salsa by adding ingredients like diced red bell pepper, black beans, or corn for additional flavors and textures.
- Adjust the spiciness by adding more or less jalapeño, depending on your heat preference.
- Ensure that the mango and avocado are ripe but not overly soft for the best texture in the salsa.

Pear and Gorgonzola Salad

Ingredients:

For the Salad:

- 4 cups mixed salad greens (e.g., arugula, spinach, or mixed baby greens)
- 2 ripe pears, thinly sliced
- 1/2 cup candied walnuts or pecans, chopped
- 1/2 cup crumbled Gorgonzola or blue cheese

For the Dressing:

- 3 tablespoons extra-virgin olive oil
- 2 tablespoons balsamic vinegar
- 1 tablespoon honey
- Salt and pepper to taste

Instructions:

Prepare Salad Greens:
- In a large salad bowl, place the mixed salad greens.

Slice Pears:
- Thinly slice the ripe pears. You can leave the skin on for added color and texture.

Add Pears to Salad:
- Arrange the sliced pears over the salad greens.

Sprinkle Nuts and Cheese:
- Sprinkle the chopped candied walnuts or pecans and crumbled Gorgonzola or blue cheese over the salad.

Make Dressing:
- In a small bowl, whisk together the extra-virgin olive oil, balsamic vinegar, honey, salt, and pepper. Adjust the quantities to achieve the desired balance of sweetness and acidity.

Drizzle Dressing:
- Drizzle the dressing over the salad. Toss the salad gently to coat the ingredients evenly with the dressing.

Serve:

- Transfer the Pear and Gorgonzola Salad to individual serving plates or a platter.

Enjoy:
- Serve immediately and enjoy this delightful combination of sweet pears, tangy Gorgonzola, and crunchy nuts!

Note:

- You can substitute other varieties of pears based on availability and preference, such as Anjou or Bosc pears.
- If you prefer a different type of cheese, such as goat cheese or feta, feel free to use that as a substitute for the Gorgonzola.
- Customize the salad by adding ingredients like dried cranberries or pomegranate seeds for extra sweetness and color.

Raspberry Chocolate Chip Cookies

Ingredients:

- 1 cup unsalted butter, softened
- 1 cup granulated sugar
- 1 cup brown sugar, packed
- 2 large eggs
- 1 teaspoon vanilla extract
- 3 cups all-purpose flour
- 1 teaspoon baking powder
- 1/2 teaspoon baking soda
- 1/2 teaspoon salt
- 1 1/2 cups semi-sweet chocolate chips
- 1 cup fresh raspberries

Instructions:

Preheat Oven:
- Preheat your oven to 350°F (175°C). Line baking sheets with parchment paper.

Cream Butter and Sugars:
- In a large mixing bowl, cream together softened butter, granulated sugar, and brown sugar until light and fluffy.

Add Eggs and Vanilla:
- Add the eggs one at a time, beating well after each addition. Stir in the vanilla extract.

Combine Dry Ingredients:
- In a separate bowl, whisk together flour, baking powder, baking soda, and salt.

Add Dry Ingredients to Wet Mixture:
- Gradually add the dry ingredients to the wet mixture, mixing until just combined. Do not overmix.

Fold in Chocolate Chips and Raspberries:
- Gently fold in the chocolate chips and fresh raspberries until evenly distributed in the cookie dough.

Scoop Dough onto Baking Sheets:
- Drop rounded tablespoons of cookie dough onto the prepared baking sheets, spacing them a few inches apart.

Bake:
- Bake in the preheated oven for 10-12 minutes or until the edges are golden brown. The centers may still look slightly soft.

Cool on Baking Sheets:
- Allow the cookies to cool on the baking sheets for 5 minutes before transferring them to wire racks to cool completely.

Serve and Enjoy:
- Once the Raspberry Chocolate Chip Cookies have cooled, serve and enjoy the delightful combination of sweet chocolate and tart raspberries in every bite!

Note:

- Be gentle when folding in the raspberries to avoid crushing them.
- If fresh raspberries are not available, you can use frozen raspberries, but be sure to pat them dry with a paper towel to remove excess moisture before adding them to the cookie dough.
- Adjust the quantity of chocolate chips and raspberries according to your taste preference.

Peach BBQ Chicken Wings

Ingredients:

For the Peach BBQ Sauce:

- 1 cup fresh or canned peaches, pureed
- 1/2 cup ketchup
- 1/4 cup brown sugar, packed
- 2 tablespoons apple cider vinegar
- 2 tablespoons Worcestershire sauce
- 1 tablespoon Dijon mustard
- 1 teaspoon garlic powder
- 1 teaspoon onion powder
- 1/2 teaspoon smoked paprika
- Salt and black pepper to taste

For the Chicken Wings:

- 2 lbs chicken wings, split at joints, tips discarded
- Salt and black pepper to taste
- 2 tablespoons vegetable oil
- Peach BBQ Sauce (for coating and dipping)
- Chopped fresh cilantro or parsley for garnish (optional)

Instructions:

Preheat Oven:
- Preheat your oven to 400°F (200°C).

Prepare Peach BBQ Sauce:
- In a blender or food processor, puree the peaches until smooth. In a saucepan, combine peach puree, ketchup, brown sugar, apple cider vinegar, Worcestershire sauce, Dijon mustard, garlic powder, onion powder, smoked paprika, salt, and black pepper. Bring to a simmer over medium heat, stirring occasionally. Cook for 10-15 minutes or until the sauce thickens. Remove from heat and set aside.

Season Chicken Wings:
- Pat the chicken wings dry with paper towels. Season them with salt and black pepper.

Bake Chicken Wings:
- Place a wire rack on a baking sheet. Arrange the seasoned chicken wings on the rack. Bake in the preheated oven for 45-50 minutes or until the wings are golden brown and crispy.

Make Peach BBQ Glaze:
- In a bowl, mix 1/2 cup of the prepared Peach BBQ Sauce with vegetable oil to create a glaze for the wings.

Coat Wings with Glaze:
- Once the wings are done baking, transfer them to a large bowl. Pour the Peach BBQ glaze over the wings and toss until they are evenly coated.

Broil (Optional):
- If you want an extra caramelized finish, you can broil the wings for an additional 2-3 minutes until they develop a slightly charred appearance. Keep a close eye to prevent burning.

Garnish and Serve:
- Arrange the Peach BBQ Chicken Wings on a serving platter. Garnish with chopped cilantro or parsley if desired.

Serve with Extra Sauce:
- Serve the wings with additional Peach BBQ Sauce on the side for dipping.

Enjoy:
- Enjoy these flavorful Peach BBQ Chicken Wings as a delicious appetizer or main dish!

Note:

- Adjust the level of spiciness by adding cayenne pepper or hot sauce to the Peach BBQ Sauce.
- You can grill the chicken wings instead of baking them for a smokier flavor. Brush the glaze on during the last few minutes of grilling.
- Ensure the wings are cooked to an internal temperature of 165°F (74°C).

Lime Coconut Energy Bites

Ingredients:

- 1 cup rolled oats
- 1/2 cup shredded coconut (plus extra for rolling)
- 1/2 cup almond butter or any nut butter of choice
- 1/3 cup honey or maple syrup
- Zest of 2 limes
- 2 tablespoons lime juice
- 1/2 teaspoon vanilla extract
- Pinch of salt

Instructions:

Combine Dry Ingredients:
- In a large bowl, combine rolled oats and shredded coconut.

Add Wet Ingredients:
- Add almond butter, honey or maple syrup, lime zest, lime juice, vanilla extract, and a pinch of salt to the dry ingredients.

Mix Well:
- Mix the ingredients thoroughly until well combined. The mixture should be sticky and easily moldable.

Chill the Mixture:
- Place the mixture in the refrigerator for about 15-30 minutes to make it easier to handle.

Roll into Bites:
- Once chilled, take small portions of the mixture and roll them into bite-sized balls using your hands.

Coat with Coconut:
- Roll each energy bite in additional shredded coconut to coat the exterior.

Chill Again (Optional):
- For a firmer texture, you can chill the energy bites in the refrigerator for an additional 15-30 minutes before serving.

Serve and Enjoy:
- Serve these Lime Coconut Energy Bites immediately, or store them in an airtight container in the refrigerator for later enjoyment.

Note:

- Customize these energy bites by adding ingredients like chia seeds, flaxseeds, or your favorite nuts for added texture and nutritional benefits.
- Adjust the sweetness by adding more or less honey or maple syrup according to your taste preference.
- Feel free to experiment with other citrus flavors by using lemon or orange zest and juice instead of lime.

Apple Cinnamon Overnight Oats

Ingredients:

- 1/2 cup rolled oats
- 1/2 cup milk (dairy or plant-based)
- 1/2 cup plain Greek yogurt
- 1/2 medium-sized apple, grated or finely chopped
- 1 tablespoon chia seeds (optional)
- 1 tablespoon honey or maple syrup
- 1/2 teaspoon ground cinnamon
- 1/4 teaspoon vanilla extract
- Pinch of salt

Instructions:

Combine Ingredients:
- In a jar or airtight container, combine rolled oats, milk, Greek yogurt, grated or chopped apple, chia seeds (if using), honey or maple syrup, ground cinnamon, vanilla extract, and a pinch of salt.

Mix Well:
- Stir the ingredients thoroughly until well combined. Make sure the oats are fully submerged in the liquid.

Refrigerate Overnight:
- Cover the jar or container and refrigerate the mixture overnight or for at least 4-6 hours. This allows the oats to absorb the liquid and soften.

Stir Before Serving:
- Before serving, give the overnight oats a good stir. If the consistency is too thick, you can add a splash of milk to reach your desired thickness.

Optional Toppings:
- Top the Apple Cinnamon Overnight Oats with additional apple slices, a sprinkle of cinnamon, chopped nuts, or a drizzle of honey before serving.

Serve and Enjoy:
- Enjoy these delicious and convenient overnight oats for a quick and nutritious breakfast!

Note:

- Adjust the sweetness by adding more or less honey or maple syrup according to your taste preference.
- Experiment with different types of apples for varying levels of sweetness and tartness.
- Feel free to customize with your favorite toppings, such as dried fruits, nuts, or seeds, for added texture and flavor.

Pomegranate Glazed Salmon

Ingredients:

For the Pomegranate Glaze:

- 1 cup pomegranate juice
- 1/4 cup honey
- 2 tablespoons soy sauce
- 1 tablespoon Dijon mustard
- 1 teaspoon grated fresh ginger
- 1 clove garlic, minced
- Salt and black pepper to taste

For the Salmon:

- 4 salmon fillets
- Salt and black pepper to taste
- 1 tablespoon olive oil
- Fresh pomegranate arils (seeds) for garnish (optional)
- Chopped fresh parsley for garnish (optional)

Instructions:

Prepare Pomegranate Glaze:
- In a small saucepan, combine pomegranate juice, honey, soy sauce, Dijon mustard, grated ginger, minced garlic, salt, and black pepper. Bring the mixture to a simmer over medium heat. Allow it to simmer for 10-15 minutes or until the glaze thickens. Remove from heat and set aside.

Preheat Oven:
- Preheat your oven to 400°F (200°C).

Season Salmon:
- Pat the salmon fillets dry with paper towels. Season them with salt and black pepper.

Sear Salmon:
- In an oven-safe skillet, heat olive oil over medium-high heat. Sear the salmon fillets, skin side down, for 2-3 minutes until golden brown.

Brush with Glaze:
- Brush the seared side of the salmon fillets with the prepared pomegranate glaze.

Bake in the Oven:
- Transfer the skillet to the preheated oven and bake for 10-12 minutes or until the salmon is cooked through and flakes easily with a fork.

Glaze Again:
- During the last few minutes of baking, brush the salmon with additional pomegranate glaze.

Garnish and Serve:
- Once the salmon is done, remove it from the oven. Garnish with fresh pomegranate arils and chopped parsley if desired.

Serve:
- Serve the Pomegranate Glazed Salmon over a bed of rice, quinoa, or your favorite side dish. Drizzle any remaining glaze over the top.

Enjoy:
- Enjoy this flavorful and elegant dish with the sweet and tangy notes of the pomegranate glaze!

Note:

- Ensure that the salmon fillets are skin-on for a crispy texture when searing.
- Adjust the sweetness and saltiness of the glaze according to your taste preference.
- Fresh herbs like thyme or rosemary can be added to the glaze for additional flavor.

Blackberry Mint Lemonade

Ingredients:

- 1 cup blackberries (fresh or frozen)
- 1/2 cup fresh mint leaves
- 1 cup freshly squeezed lemon juice (about 4-6 lemons)
- 1/2 cup honey or to taste
- 4 cups cold water
- Ice cubes
- Fresh blackberries, mint sprigs, and lemon slices for garnish (optional)

Instructions:

Prepare Simple Syrup:
- In a small saucepan, combine 1/2 cup of water and honey. Heat over medium heat, stirring, until the honey is fully dissolved. Remove from heat and let it cool.

Blend Blackberries and Mint:
- In a blender, combine blackberries, mint leaves, and the cooled honey syrup. Blend until smooth.

Strain the Mixture:
- Strain the blackberry-mint mixture through a fine mesh sieve or cheesecloth into a pitcher to remove seeds and pulp. Press down to extract as much liquid as possible.

Add Lemon Juice:
- Stir in the freshly squeezed lemon juice into the strained blackberry-mint mixture.

Mix with Water:
- Add cold water to the pitcher and mix well. Adjust the sweetness by adding more honey if needed.

Chill:
- Refrigerate the blackberry mint lemonade for at least 1-2 hours to allow the flavors to meld.

Serve Over Ice:
- When ready to serve, fill glasses with ice cubes and pour the blackberry mint lemonade over the ice.

Garnish (Optional):

- Garnish each glass with fresh blackberries, mint sprigs, and lemon slices if desired.

Stir Before Serving:
- Give the lemonade a gentle stir before serving to distribute the flavors.

Enjoy:
- Enjoy this refreshing and vibrant Blackberry Mint Lemonade on a hot day or as a delightful party beverage!

Note:

- Adjust the sweetness and tartness by varying the amount of honey and lemon juice to suit your taste.
- For a sparkling version, you can top the lemonade with sparkling water or club soda.
- This recipe can be easily adapted with other berries like raspberries or blueberries for different flavor variations.

Caramel Apple Crisp

Ingredients:

For the Apple Filling:

- 6 cups peeled and sliced apples (such as Granny Smith or Honeycrisp)
- 1/4 cup granulated sugar
- 2 tablespoons all-purpose flour
- 1 teaspoon ground cinnamon
- 1/4 teaspoon ground nutmeg
- 1/4 teaspoon salt
- 2 tablespoons caramel sauce (plus extra for serving, if desired)

For the Crisp Topping:

- 1 cup old-fashioned rolled oats
- 1/2 cup all-purpose flour
- 1/2 cup brown sugar, packed
- 1/4 teaspoon baking powder
- 1/4 teaspoon ground cinnamon
- 1/2 cup unsalted butter, melted

Optional Garnish:

- Vanilla ice cream or whipped cream

Instructions:

Preheat Oven:
- Preheat your oven to 350°F (175°C). Grease a baking dish (approximately 9x9 inches or a similar size).

Prepare Apple Filling:
- In a large bowl, combine the sliced apples, granulated sugar, flour, cinnamon, nutmeg, salt, and 2 tablespoons of caramel sauce. Toss until the apples are evenly coated.

Transfer to Baking Dish:

- Transfer the apple mixture to the greased baking dish, spreading it out evenly.

Make Crisp Topping:
- In a separate bowl, mix together the rolled oats, flour, brown sugar, baking powder, and cinnamon. Pour the melted butter over the dry ingredients and stir until well combined.

Spread Topping Over Apples:
- Sprinkle the crisp topping evenly over the apple mixture in the baking dish, covering the apples completely.

Bake:
- Bake in the preheated oven for 40-45 minutes or until the topping is golden brown, and the apples are tender and bubbling.

Cool Slightly:
- Allow the caramel apple crisp to cool slightly before serving.

Serve and Garnish:
- Serve the caramel apple crisp warm. Drizzle additional caramel sauce over the top if desired. Garnish with a scoop of vanilla ice cream or a dollop of whipped cream for an extra indulgence.

Enjoy:
- Enjoy the delicious combination of sweet, spiced apples and crunchy oat topping in this comforting caramel apple crisp!

Note:

- You can adjust the level of sweetness by adding more or less sugar to the apple filling.
- Experiment with different apple varieties for varying flavors and textures in the crisp.
- Serve leftovers warm or reheat before enjoying to maintain the crisp texture.

Mango Chili Lime Chicken Tacos

Ingredients:

For the Mango Chili Lime Chicken:

- 1 pound boneless, skinless chicken breasts, thinly sliced
- 2 tablespoons olive oil
- 2 tablespoons chili powder
- 1 teaspoon ground cumin
- 1 teaspoon smoked paprika
- 1 teaspoon garlic powder
- Salt and black pepper to taste
- Zest and juice of 2 limes
- 1 tablespoon honey
- 1 ripe mango, peeled, pitted, and diced

For Assembling Tacos:

- 8 small flour or corn tortillas, warmed
- Shredded lettuce or cabbage
- Diced tomatoes
- Red onion, thinly sliced
- Fresh cilantro, chopped
- Lime wedges for serving

Instructions:

Marinate Chicken:
- In a bowl, combine sliced chicken with olive oil, chili powder, cumin, smoked paprika, garlic powder, salt, black pepper, lime zest, lime juice, and honey. Mix well, ensuring the chicken is evenly coated. Marinate for at least 15-20 minutes.

Cook Chicken:
- Heat a skillet over medium-high heat. Add the marinated chicken slices and cook for 5-7 minutes or until the chicken is fully cooked and slightly charred. Stir in diced mango during the last 2 minutes of cooking.

Assemble Tacos:
- Warm the tortillas in a dry skillet or microwave. Place a spoonful of the mango chili lime chicken onto each tortilla.

Add Toppings:
- Top the chicken with shredded lettuce or cabbage, diced tomatoes, thinly sliced red onion, and chopped cilantro.

Serve:
- Serve the Mango Chili Lime Chicken Tacos with lime wedges on the side.

Enjoy:
- Enjoy these vibrant and flavorful tacos with the sweet and spicy kick of mango chili lime chicken!

Note:

- Customize your toppings based on personal preference. Add ingredients like avocado slices, salsa, or cheese.
- Adjust the level of spiciness by increasing or decreasing the amount of chili powder.
- For an extra burst of flavor, drizzle additional lime juice over the assembled tacos before serving.

Pear Gingerbread Loaf

Ingredients:

- 2 cups all-purpose flour
- 1 teaspoon baking soda
- 1/2 teaspoon baking powder
- 1/2 teaspoon salt
- 1 teaspoon ground ginger
- 1 teaspoon ground cinnamon
- 1/2 teaspoon ground nutmeg
- 1/4 teaspoon ground cloves
- 1/2 cup unsalted butter, softened
- 1/2 cup granulated sugar
- 1/2 cup brown sugar, packed
- 2 large eggs
- 1 teaspoon vanilla extract
- 1 cup unsweetened applesauce
- 1 cup ripe pears, peeled and diced

Instructions:

Preheat Oven:
- Preheat your oven to 350°F (175°C). Grease and flour a 9x5-inch loaf pan.

Combine Dry Ingredients:
- In a medium bowl, whisk together flour, baking soda, baking powder, salt, ground ginger, ground cinnamon, ground nutmeg, and ground cloves. Set aside.

Cream Butter and Sugars:
- In a large bowl, cream together softened butter, granulated sugar, and brown sugar until light and fluffy.

Add Eggs and Vanilla:
- Add the eggs one at a time, beating well after each addition. Stir in the vanilla extract.

Add Dry Ingredients:
- Gradually add the dry ingredients to the wet mixture, mixing until just combined. Do not overmix.

Add Applesauce and Pears:

- Fold in the unsweetened applesauce until well incorporated. Gently fold in the diced ripe pears.

Transfer to Loaf Pan:
- Pour the batter into the prepared loaf pan, spreading it evenly.

Bake:
- Bake in the preheated oven for 55-65 minutes or until a toothpick inserted into the center comes out clean or with a few moist crumbs.

Cool:
- Allow the pear gingerbread loaf to cool in the pan for about 10 minutes, then transfer it to a wire rack to cool completely.

Slice and Serve:
- Once completely cooled, slice the pear gingerbread loaf and serve. Optionally, dust with powdered sugar or drizzle with a simple glaze.

Enjoy:
- Enjoy this moist and flavorful Pear Gingerbread Loaf with a warm cup of tea or coffee!

Note:

- Adjust the spices to your preference, adding more or less ginger, cinnamon, or nutmeg.
- If you prefer a glaze, you can mix powdered sugar with a little milk or lemon juice and drizzle it over the cooled loaf.

Citrus Shrimp Skewers

Ingredients:

For the Marinade:

- 1/4 cup olive oil
- 1/4 cup fresh orange juice
- 2 tablespoons fresh lemon juice
- 2 tablespoons fresh lime juice
- 2 cloves garlic, minced
- 1 teaspoon honey
- 1 teaspoon Dijon mustard
- 1 teaspoon paprika
- Salt and black pepper to taste

For the Shrimp Skewers:

- 1 pound large shrimp, peeled and deveined
- Wooden or metal skewers (if using wooden skewers, soak them in water for at least 30 minutes)

For Garnish (optional):

- Fresh cilantro, chopped
- Orange, lemon, and lime slices

Instructions:

Prepare Marinade:
- In a bowl, whisk together olive oil, fresh orange juice, fresh lemon juice, fresh lime juice, minced garlic, honey, Dijon mustard, paprika, salt, and black pepper. This is your citrus marinade.

Marinate Shrimp:
- Place the peeled and deveined shrimp in a resealable plastic bag or shallow dish. Pour the citrus marinade over the shrimp, ensuring they are

well-coated. Marinate in the refrigerator for at least 30 minutes, allowing the flavors to infuse.

Preheat Grill:
- Preheat your grill or grill pan to medium-high heat.

Skewer Shrimp:
- Thread the marinated shrimp onto the skewers, evenly dividing them.

Grill Shrimp:
- Grill the shrimp skewers for 2-3 minutes per side or until the shrimp are opaque and slightly charred.

Garnish (Optional):
- Garnish the citrus shrimp skewers with chopped fresh cilantro and serve with slices of orange, lemon, and lime for an extra burst of citrus flavor.

Serve:
- Arrange the citrus shrimp skewers on a platter and serve immediately.

Enjoy:
- Enjoy these delicious and zesty Citrus Shrimp Skewers as a flavorful appetizer or main dish!

Note:

- You can add a pinch of red pepper flakes to the marinade for a hint of spice.
- Serve the skewers over a bed of rice, couscous, or a salad for a complete meal.
- Feel free to customize the marinade with additional herbs and spices to suit your taste.

Blueberry Balsamic Glazed Chicken

Ingredients:

For the Blueberry Balsamic Glaze:

- 1 cup fresh or frozen blueberries
- 1/4 cup balsamic vinegar
- 2 tablespoons honey
- 1 tablespoon Dijon mustard
- 1 clove garlic, minced
- Salt and black pepper to taste

For the Chicken:

- 4 boneless, skinless chicken breasts
- Salt and black pepper to taste
- 2 tablespoons olive oil
- Fresh basil or mint leaves for garnish (optional)

Instructions:

Prepare Blueberry Balsamic Glaze:
- In a saucepan, combine blueberries, balsamic vinegar, honey, Dijon mustard, minced garlic, salt, and black pepper. Bring the mixture to a simmer over medium heat.

Simmer and Mash Blueberries:
- Simmer the blueberry mixture for 10-12 minutes, mashing the blueberries with the back of a spoon or a potato masher. Continue simmering until the mixture thickens to a glaze-like consistency.

Strain (Optional):
- For a smoother glaze, you can strain the blueberry mixture through a fine mesh sieve to remove any remaining solids. This step is optional, and you can leave the blueberry bits if desired.

Season Chicken:
- Season the chicken breasts with salt and black pepper.

Cook Chicken:

- In a large skillet, heat olive oil over medium-high heat. Add the seasoned chicken breasts and cook for 5-7 minutes per side or until fully cooked and golden brown.

Glaze Chicken:
- Pour the blueberry balsamic glaze over the cooked chicken breasts, coating them evenly. Allow the glaze to simmer with the chicken for an additional 2-3 minutes.

Garnish (Optional):
- Garnish the Blueberry Balsamic Glazed Chicken with fresh basil or mint leaves for added freshness.

Serve:
- Transfer the glazed chicken to serving plates and spoon any additional glaze over the top.

Enjoy:
- Enjoy this delightful Blueberry Balsamic Glazed Chicken with a side of rice, quinoa, or your favorite vegetables!

Note:

- Adjust the sweetness and tanginess of the glaze by adding more honey or balsamic vinegar according to your taste preference.
- Experiment with different herbs in the glaze or for garnish, such as thyme or rosemary.
- Fresh or frozen blueberries can be used for the glaze, depending on availability.

Apricot Glazed Pork Chops

Ingredients:

For the Apricot Glaze:

- 1/2 cup apricot preserves
- 2 tablespoons soy sauce
- 2 tablespoons Dijon mustard
- 1 tablespoon honey
- 1 tablespoon apple cider vinegar
- 1 teaspoon minced garlic
- 1/2 teaspoon ground ginger
- Salt and black pepper to taste

For the Pork Chops:

- 4 bone-in pork chops
- Salt and black pepper to taste
- 2 tablespoons olive oil
- Fresh parsley for garnish (optional)

Instructions:

Preheat Oven:
- Preheat your oven to 375°F (190°C).

Prepare Apricot Glaze:
- In a small saucepan, combine apricot preserves, soy sauce, Dijon mustard, honey, apple cider vinegar, minced garlic, ground ginger, salt, and black pepper. Heat over medium heat, stirring, until the preserves melt and the ingredients are well combined. Simmer for 3-5 minutes until the glaze thickens slightly. Set aside.

Season Pork Chops:
- Season the pork chops with salt and black pepper.

Sear Pork Chops:
- In an oven-safe skillet, heat olive oil over medium-high heat. Sear the pork chops for 2-3 minutes on each side until golden brown.

Brush with Apricot Glaze:
- Brush the apricot glaze over each pork chop, coating them generously.

Bake in the Oven:
- Transfer the skillet to the preheated oven and bake for 15-20 minutes or until the internal temperature of the pork reaches 145°F (63°C) for medium doneness.

Baste During Cooking:
- Optionally, baste the pork chops with additional apricot glaze during the baking process for extra flavor.

Rest Before Serving:
- Allow the pork chops to rest for a few minutes before serving. This helps the juices redistribute for a juicier result.

Garnish (Optional):
- Garnish the Apricot-Glazed Pork Chops with fresh parsley if desired.

Serve:
- Serve the glazed pork chops with your favorite sides, such as roasted vegetables, rice, or mashed potatoes.

Enjoy:
- Enjoy these succulent Apricot-Glazed Pork Chops with a perfect balance of sweet and savory flavors!

Note:

- Adjust the sweetness and saltiness of the glaze according to your taste preference.
- If you don't have an oven-safe skillet, you can transfer the seared pork chops to a baking dish before brushing them with the apricot glaze and baking in the oven.
- Ensure the pork chops reach a safe internal temperature of 145°F (63°C) for medium doneness.

Mixed Fruit Galette

Ingredients:

For the Galette Dough:

- 1 1/4 cups all-purpose flour
- 1 tablespoon granulated sugar
- 1/2 teaspoon salt
- 1/2 cup unsalted butter, cold and cut into small cubes
- 3-4 tablespoons ice water

For the Mixed Fruit Filling:

- 2 cups mixed fresh fruits (such as berries, peaches, plums, or apples), sliced or diced
- 2 tablespoons granulated sugar
- 1 tablespoon cornstarch
- 1 teaspoon vanilla extract
- Zest of 1 lemon

For Brushing and Sprinkling:

- 1 egg, beaten (for egg wash)
- 1 tablespoon turbinado sugar (or granulated sugar) for sprinkling

Instructions:

Prepare the Galette Dough:

Combine Dry Ingredients:
- In a food processor, combine the flour, sugar, and salt. Pulse a few times to mix.

Add Cold Butter:
- Add the cold, cubed butter to the flour mixture. Pulse until the mixture resembles coarse crumbs.

Add Ice Water:
- With the processor running, gradually add the ice water, one tablespoon at a time, until the dough just comes together.

Form Dough:

- Turn the dough out onto a floured surface. Shape it into a disk, wrap it in plastic wrap, and refrigerate for at least 30 minutes.

Prepare the Fruit Filling:

Preheat Oven:
- Preheat your oven to 375°F (190°C).

Mix Fruit Filling:
- In a bowl, gently toss together the mixed fruits, granulated sugar, cornstarch, vanilla extract, and lemon zest until well combined.

Assemble the Galette:

Roll Out Dough:
- On a floured surface, roll out the chilled galette dough into a circle of about 12 inches in diameter.

Transfer to Baking Sheet:
- Carefully transfer the rolled-out dough to a parchment-lined baking sheet.

Arrange Fruit Filling:
- Arrange the mixed fruit filling in the center of the rolled-out dough, leaving a border around the edges.

Fold and Crimp Edges:
- Fold the edges of the dough over the fruit, crimping as you go to create a rustic, free-form shape.

Brush with Egg Wash:
- Brush the edges of the galette with the beaten egg to give it a golden finish.

Sprinkle with Sugar:
- Sprinkle the turbinado sugar (or granulated sugar) over the brushed edges.

Bake the Galette:

Bake in the Oven:
- Bake in the preheated oven for 30-35 minutes or until the crust is golden brown, and the fruit is bubbly.

Cool Before Serving:
- Allow the mixed fruit galette to cool slightly before serving.

Serve and Enjoy:

- Serve the galette warm or at room temperature. Enjoy it on its own or with a scoop of vanilla ice cream.

Note:

- Feel free to customize the fruit filling based on your preference and seasonal availability.
- Adjust the sweetness of the filling by adding more or less sugar according to your taste.

Honeydew Basil Granita

Ingredients:

- 1 medium-sized honeydew melon, peeled, seeded, and diced (about 4 cups)
- 1/2 cup fresh basil leaves, packed
- 1/3 cup honey (adjust to taste)
- 1/4 cup fresh lime juice
- 1/2 cup water

Instructions:

Prepare Honeydew and Basil:
- Peel, seed, and dice the honeydew melon. Ensure it is ripe and sweet.

Blend Ingredients:
- In a blender, combine the diced honeydew melon, fresh basil leaves, honey, fresh lime juice, and water. Blend until smooth and well combined.

Strain Mixture (Optional):
- If you prefer a smoother texture, you can strain the mixture using a fine mesh sieve to remove any pulp. This step is optional.

Pour into a Pan:
- Pour the blended mixture into a shallow, wide pan or dish.

Freeze:
- Place the pan in the freezer. Every 30 minutes, use a fork to scrape and stir the mixture to create a granular texture. Continue this process for about 3-4 hours or until the granita has a slushy consistency.

Serve:
- Once the honeydew basil granita is fully frozen and has a light, fluffy texture, it's ready to be served.

Garnish (Optional):
- Garnish the honeydew basil granita with fresh basil leaves before serving.

Serve and Enjoy:
- Scoop the granita into bowls or glasses and enjoy this refreshing and subtly sweet frozen treat.

Note:

- Adjust the sweetness by adding more or less honey, depending on your preference and the sweetness of the honeydew melon.

- You can experiment with different herbs like mint or a combination of herbs for unique flavor variations.
- Serve the honeydew basil granita as a palate cleanser between courses or as a light and refreshing dessert.

Pear and Walnut Salad

Ingredients:

For the Salad:

- 4 cups mixed salad greens (e.g., arugula, spinach, or mixed greens)
- 2 ripe pears, cored and thinly sliced
- 1/2 cup crumbled blue cheese or feta cheese
- 1/2 cup chopped walnuts, toasted
- 1/4 cup dried cranberries or pomegranate arils (optional)
- Freshly ground black pepper, to taste

For the Dressing:

- 1/4 cup extra-virgin olive oil
- 2 tablespoons balsamic vinegar
- 1 tablespoon honey
- 1 teaspoon Dijon mustard
- Salt and pepper to taste

Instructions:

Prepare the Salad:

Toast Walnuts:
- In a dry skillet over medium heat, toast the chopped walnuts for a few minutes until fragrant. Be careful not to burn them. Set aside to cool.

Assemble Salad:
- In a large salad bowl, combine the mixed salad greens, thinly sliced pears, crumbled blue cheese or feta, toasted walnuts, and dried cranberries or pomegranate arils if using.

Prepare the Dressing:

Whisk Dressing:

- In a small bowl, whisk together the extra-virgin olive oil, balsamic vinegar, honey, Dijon mustard, salt, and pepper until well combined.

Dress the Salad:
- Drizzle the dressing over the salad just before serving. Toss gently to coat the ingredients evenly.

Season with Pepper:
- Add freshly ground black pepper to taste. Adjust the salt and pepper as needed.

Serve:
- Serve the Pear and Walnut Salad immediately as a refreshing and flavorful side dish.

Note:

- Feel free to customize the salad with additional ingredients like sliced red onions, avocado, or goat cheese based on your preferences.
- Adjust the sweetness and acidity of the dressing by adding more honey or balsamic vinegar, according to your taste.
- Pecans or almonds can be used instead of walnuts if preferred.

Coconut Pineapple Popsicles

Ingredients:

- 1 cup coconut milk
- 1 cup pineapple chunks (fresh or canned)
- 2 tablespoons honey or agave syrup (adjust to taste)
- 1 teaspoon vanilla extract
- Pinch of salt

Instructions:

Blend Ingredients:
- In a blender, combine coconut milk, pineapple chunks, honey or agave syrup, vanilla extract, and a pinch of salt.

Blend Until Smooth:
- Blend the ingredients until you have a smooth and well-combined mixture.

Taste and Adjust Sweetness:
- Taste the mixture and adjust the sweetness by adding more honey or agave syrup if needed.

Pour into Popsicle Molds:
- Pour the coconut pineapple mixture into popsicle molds, leaving a little space at the top for expansion.

Insert Popsicle Sticks:
- Insert popsicle sticks into the molds. If your molds come with a cover, secure them to keep the sticks in place.

Freeze:
- Place the popsicle molds in the freezer and let them freeze for at least 4-6 hours or until completely solid.

Run Molds Under Warm Water:
- Before unmolding, run the popsicle molds under warm water for a few seconds. This helps in releasing the popsicles easily.

Serve and Enjoy:
- Once unmolded, serve the Coconut Pineapple Popsicles immediately and enjoy this tropical and refreshing frozen treat!

Note:

- Feel free to add shredded coconut or chunks of fresh pineapple to the popsicle molds for added texture.
- Adjust the coconut milk to pineapple ratio based on your preference for a more coconut-forward or pineapple-forward flavor.
- If you don't have popsicle molds, you can use small cups and insert wooden sticks. Cover the cups with foil and make a small slit for the stick to hold it in place.

Citrus Avocado Quinoa Salad

Ingredients:

For the Salad:

- 1 cup quinoa, cooked and cooled
- 2 ripe avocados, diced
- 1 cup cherry tomatoes, halved
- 1/2 cucumber, diced
- 1/4 cup red onion, finely chopped
- 1/4 cup fresh cilantro, chopped
- 1/4 cup feta cheese, crumbled (optional)
- Salt and black pepper to taste

For the Citrus Dressing:

- 1/4 cup extra-virgin olive oil
- 2 tablespoons fresh orange juice
- 1 tablespoon fresh lemon juice
- 1 teaspoon honey
- 1 teaspoon Dijon mustard
- Salt and black pepper to taste

Instructions:

Prepare the Salad:

    Cook Quinoa:
- Cook quinoa according to package instructions. Once cooked, let it cool.

    Dice Avocados:
- Dice the ripe avocados and place them in a large salad bowl.

    Prepare Vegetables:
- Add cherry tomatoes (halved), diced cucumber, finely chopped red onion, and chopped fresh cilantro to the bowl.

    Add Quinoa:
- Add the cooled quinoa to the bowl with the vegetables.

    Optional Feta Cheese:
- If using feta cheese, crumble it over the salad ingredients.

    Season:

- Season the salad with salt and black pepper to taste.

Prepare the Citrus Dressing:

Whisk Dressing:
- In a small bowl, whisk together extra-virgin olive oil, fresh orange juice, fresh lemon juice, honey, Dijon mustard, salt, and black pepper until well combined.

Dress the Salad:
- Pour the citrus dressing over the salad ingredients.

Toss Gently:
- Gently toss the salad to ensure all ingredients are well coated with the dressing.

Chill (Optional):
- If time allows, refrigerate the Citrus Avocado Quinoa Salad for about 30 minutes to allow the flavors to meld.

Serve:
- Serve the salad in individual bowls or as a side dish for a refreshing and nutritious meal.

Note:

- Customize the salad by adding other ingredients like grilled chicken, shrimp, or chickpeas for added protein.
- Adjust the sweetness and acidity of the dressing by tweaking the amount of honey and citrus juices.
- Feel free to experiment with different herbs and spices based on your taste preferences.

Cherry Almond Clafoutis

Ingredients:

- 1 cup fresh cherries, pitted and halved
- 1/2 cup slivered almonds
- 3 large eggs
- 1 cup whole milk
- 1/2 cup all-purpose flour
- 1/2 cup granulated sugar
- 1 teaspoon almond extract
- 1/4 teaspoon salt
- Powdered sugar, for dusting (optional)
- Sliced almonds, for garnish (optional)

Instructions:

Preheat Oven:
- Preheat your oven to 350°F (180°C). Grease a baking dish or tart pan.

Prepare Cherries:
- Pit the cherries and cut them in half. Arrange the cherry halves in a single layer in the greased baking dish.

Sprinkle with Almonds:
- Sprinkle the slivered almonds over the cherries in the baking dish.

Prepare Batter:
- In a blender, combine eggs, whole milk, all-purpose flour, granulated sugar, almond extract, and salt. Blend until the batter is smooth.

Pour Batter Over Cherries:
- Pour the batter over the cherries and almonds in the baking dish.

Bake:
- Bake in the preheated oven for 35-40 minutes or until the clafoutis is set and golden brown on top.

Cool Slightly:
- Allow the cherry almond clafoutis to cool slightly before serving.

Dust with Powdered Sugar (Optional):
- Dust the clafoutis with powdered sugar just before serving for a decorative touch.

Garnish with Sliced Almonds (Optional):

- Optionally, garnish with additional sliced almonds for extra crunch and visual appeal.

Serve:
- Serve the cherry almond clafoutis warm. It can be enjoyed on its own or with a dollop of whipped cream or a scoop of vanilla ice cream.

Enjoy:
- Enjoy this classic French dessert with the delightful combination of cherries and almonds!

Note:

- Clafoutis is traditionally made with whole cherries, including the pits, as they are believed to impart additional flavor to the dish. However, pitting the cherries is a common modern practice for ease of eating.
- Feel free to experiment with other fruits or nuts in the clafoutis based on your preferences.

Lemon Raspberry Thumbprint Cookies

Ingredients:

For the Cookies:

- 1 cup unsalted butter, softened
- 1/2 cup granulated sugar
- 2 large egg yolks
- 1 teaspoon vanilla extract
- 2 cups all-purpose flour
- 1/4 teaspoon salt
- Zest of 1 lemon

For the Raspberry Filling:

- 1/2 cup raspberry jam or preserves

For the Lemon Glaze:

- 1 cup powdered sugar
- 2 tablespoons fresh lemon juice
- Zest of 1 lemon

Instructions:

Prepare the Cookies:

Preheat Oven:
- Preheat your oven to 350°F (180°C). Line a baking sheet with parchment paper.

Cream Butter and Sugar:
- In a large bowl, cream together the softened butter and granulated sugar until light and fluffy.

Add Egg Yolks and Vanilla:
- Add the egg yolks and vanilla extract to the butter mixture. Mix until well combined.

Add Dry Ingredients:
- In a separate bowl, whisk together the all-purpose flour and salt. Gradually add this dry mixture to the wet ingredients, mixing just until combined. Fold in the lemon zest.

Form Cookie Dough Balls:
- Roll the cookie dough into 1-inch balls and place them on the prepared baking sheet, spacing them about 2 inches apart.

Create Thumbprints:
- Use your thumb or the back of a teaspoon to make an indentation in the center of each cookie.

Fill with Raspberry Jam:
- Spoon a small amount of raspberry jam into each thumbprint indentation.

Bake:
- Bake in the preheated oven for 12-15 minutes or until the edges of the cookies are lightly golden.

Cool:
- Allow the cookies to cool on the baking sheet for a few minutes before transferring them to a wire rack to cool completely.

Prepare the Lemon Glaze:

Whisk Glaze Ingredients:
- In a bowl, whisk together the powdered sugar, fresh lemon juice, and lemon zest until smooth.

Glaze Cookies:
- Once the cookies are completely cooled, drizzle each cookie with the lemon glaze.

Allow Glaze to Set:
- Allow the lemon glaze to set before serving or storing the cookies.

Serve and Enjoy:
- Serve these delightful Lemon Raspberry Thumbprint Cookies and enjoy the burst of citrus and fruity flavors!

Note:

- Feel free to experiment with different fruit preserves or jams for the thumbprint filling.

- Adjust the amount of lemon juice and zest in the glaze to suit your taste preferences.

Plum Ginger Chutney

Ingredients:

- 2 cups ripe plums, pitted and chopped
- 1/2 cup red onion, finely chopped
- 1/4 cup fresh ginger, peeled and minced
- 1/2 cup brown sugar
- 1/4 cup apple cider vinegar
- 1/4 cup raisins
- 1 teaspoon mustard seeds
- 1/2 teaspoon ground cinnamon
- 1/4 teaspoon ground cloves
- 1/4 teaspoon red pepper flakes (optional for heat)
- Salt to taste

Instructions:

Prepare Ingredients:
- Pit and chop the plums, finely chop the red onion, peel and mince the fresh ginger.

Cook Plums and Onions:
- In a medium saucepan over medium heat, combine the chopped plums, finely chopped red onion, and minced ginger. Cook for a few minutes until the onions are softened.

Add Remaining Ingredients:
- Add brown sugar, apple cider vinegar, raisins, mustard seeds, ground cinnamon, ground cloves, and red pepper flakes (if using) to the saucepan. Stir well to combine.

Simmer:
- Bring the mixture to a simmer and then reduce the heat to low. Let it simmer for about 25-30 minutes or until the chutney thickens, and the flavors meld. Stir occasionally.

Adjust Seasoning:
- Taste the chutney and adjust the seasoning. Add salt to taste.

Cool:
- Remove the saucepan from heat and let the plum ginger chutney cool to room temperature.

Store:
- Transfer the chutney to sterilized jars and store in the refrigerator.

Serve:
- Serve the Plum Ginger Chutney as a condiment with grilled meats, cheese, or as a flavorful accompaniment to various dishes.

Note:

- Adjust the sweetness and tartness of the chutney by modifying the amount of brown sugar and apple cider vinegar according to your taste preferences.
- Feel free to add a pinch of ground nutmeg or allspice for additional warm and aromatic flavors.
- This chutney can be stored in the refrigerator for several weeks.

Blood Orange Sorbet

Ingredients:

- 2 cups fresh blood orange juice (about 8-10 blood oranges)
- 3/4 cup granulated sugar
- 1/2 cup water
- 1 tablespoon fresh lemon juice

Instructions:

Juice Blood Oranges:
- Squeeze the juice from the blood oranges to obtain about 2 cups of fresh juice. Strain the juice to remove any pulp or seeds.

Make Simple Syrup:
- In a small saucepan, combine granulated sugar and water. Heat over medium heat, stirring occasionally, until the sugar is completely dissolved. Allow the simple syrup to cool.

Combine Ingredients:
- In a bowl, mix the fresh blood orange juice, cooled simple syrup, and fresh lemon juice. Stir until well combined.

Chill Mixture:
- Place the mixture in the refrigerator to chill for at least 2 hours or until thoroughly chilled.

Freeze in Ice Cream Maker:
- Pour the chilled blood orange mixture into an ice cream maker and churn according to the manufacturer's instructions until it reaches a slushy, sorbet consistency.

Transfer to Container:
- Transfer the sorbet to a lidded container, spreading it evenly. Cover the surface with parchment paper or plastic wrap to prevent ice crystals from forming.

Freeze Until Firm:
- Freeze the blood orange sorbet for an additional 4-6 hours or overnight until it is firm.

Serve and Enjoy:
- Scoop the blood orange sorbet into bowls or cones and enjoy this refreshing and citrusy frozen treat.

Note:

- If you don't have an ice cream maker, you can pour the chilled mixture into a shallow dish, cover it, and place it in the freezer. Every 30 minutes, stir the mixture with a fork to break up ice crystals until it reaches a sorbet consistency.
- Adjust the sweetness by adding more or less sugar, depending on your preference and the sweetness of the blood oranges.
- Garnish with fresh mint or a slice of blood orange for an extra touch of elegance when serving.

Papaya Coconut Smoothie

Ingredients:

- 1 cup ripe papaya, peeled, seeded, and diced
- 1/2 cup coconut milk
- 1/2 cup plain or vanilla yogurt
- 1 tablespoon honey or agave syrup (optional, depending on sweetness preference)
- 1/2 cup ice cubes
- Unsweetened shredded coconut, for garnish (optional)

Instructions:

Prepare Papaya:
- Peel, seed, and dice the ripe papaya.

Combine Ingredients:
- In a blender, combine the diced papaya, coconut milk, yogurt, honey or agave syrup (if using), and ice cubes.

Blend Until Smooth:
- Blend the ingredients until smooth and well combined. If the smoothie is too thick, you can add more coconut milk or water to achieve the desired consistency.

Taste and Adjust Sweetness:
- Taste the smoothie and adjust the sweetness by adding more honey or agave syrup if needed.

Serve:
- Pour the papaya coconut smoothie into glasses.

Garnish (Optional):
- If desired, garnish the smoothie with a sprinkle of unsweetened shredded coconut for added texture.

Serve and Enjoy:
- Serve the Papaya Coconut Smoothie immediately and enjoy this tropical and refreshing beverage!

Note:

- To make the smoothie colder without diluting it with more ice, you can freeze the diced papaya before blending.

- Experiment with the ratio of coconut milk and yogurt based on your preference for a creamier or lighter texture.
- For an extra nutritional boost, you can add a handful of spinach or kale to the blender without significantly affecting the flavor.

Cinnamon Sugar Baked Apples

Ingredients:

- 4 large baking apples (such as Honeycrisp or Granny Smith)
- 1/4 cup unsalted butter, melted
- 1/4 cup brown sugar
- 1 teaspoon ground cinnamon
- 1/4 teaspoon ground nutmeg
- 1/4 cup chopped nuts (such as walnuts or pecans), optional
- Vanilla ice cream or whipped cream, for serving (optional)

Instructions:

Preheat Oven:
- Preheat your oven to 375°F (190°C).

Prepare Apples:
- Wash and core the apples, leaving the bottoms intact. You can use an apple corer or a knife to remove the cores while keeping the apples whole.

Make Cinnamon Sugar Mixture:
- In a small bowl, mix together melted butter, brown sugar, ground cinnamon, and ground nutmeg to create the cinnamon sugar mixture.

Coat Apples:
- Place the cored apples in a baking dish. Brush the apples with the cinnamon sugar mixture, making sure to coat them evenly.

Optional: Add Nuts:
- If using chopped nuts, sprinkle them over the tops of the apples, pressing them gently into the cinnamon sugar mixture.

Bake:
- Bake the apples in the preheated oven for 25-30 minutes or until they are tender but not mushy. The baking time may vary depending on the size and type of apples.

Baste:
- During baking, baste the apples with the juices from the bottom of the baking dish a couple of times to enhance the flavor.

Serve:
- Remove the baked apples from the oven and let them cool slightly before serving.

Optional: Serve with Ice Cream or Whipped Cream:

- Serve the cinnamon sugar baked apples warm. They can be enjoyed on their own or with a scoop of vanilla ice cream or a dollop of whipped cream.

Enjoy:
- Enjoy the comforting and aromatic flavors of these cinnamon sugar baked apples!

Note:

- Adjust the sweetness by adding more or less brown sugar to the cinnamon sugar mixture, depending on your preference and the natural sweetness of the apples.
- You can customize the filling by adding raisins, dried cranberries, or other dried fruits to the cinnamon sugar mixture.
- Experiment with different apple varieties to find your favorite for baking.

www.ingramcontent.com/pod-product-compliance
Lightning Source LLC
LaVergne TN
LVHW061943070526
838199LV00060B/3941